Understanding Shared Services in Early Childhood Education

Redleaf *Quick* Guide

Understanding Shared Services in Early Childhood Education

Amanda L. Krause-DiScala, EdM

Redleaf Press®
www.redleafpress.org
800-423-8309

Published by Redleaf Press
10 Yorkton Court
St. Paul, MN 55117
www.redleafpress.org

First edition 2023
Cover design by Renee Hammes
Cover photograph by peopleimages.com / stock.adobe.com
Typeset in Signo and Avenir by Douglas Schmitz

Printed in the United States of America
30 29 28 27 26 25 24 23   1 2 3 4 5 6 7 8

Library of Congress Cataloging-in-Publication Data

Names: Krause-DiScala, Amanda L., author.
Title: Understanding shared services in early childhood education / by
  Amanda L. Krause-DiScala.
Description: First Edition. | St. Paul, MN : Redleaf Press, [2023] |
  Includes bibliographical references. | Summary: "Shared services
  knowledge hubs and alliances together allow us to collaborate with other
  professionals and save time and money, focusing these resources instead
  on increasing quality, addressing workforce issues, and expanding access
  of services to children and families with fewer barriers. Understanding
  Shared Services in Early Childhood Education, a Redleaf Quick Guide,
  explains how leveraging shared services systems can help through pooling
  resources and information and sharing access to technology such as
  automation and financial management systems"—Provided by publisher.
Identifiers: LCCN 2022041658 (print) | LCCN 2022041659 (ebook) | ISBN
  9781605547879 (Paperback : acid-free paper) | ISBN 9781605547886 (eBook)

Subjects: LCSH: Early childhood education. | Shared services (Management)
Classification: LCC LB1139.23 .K73 2023 (print) | LCC LB1139.23 (ebook) |
  DDC 372.21068--dc23/eng/20221025
LC record available at https://lccn.loc.gov/2022041658
LC ebook record available at https://lccn.loc.gov/2022041659

Printed on acid-free paper

For Ella, Jake, Lily, Grace, and Nina.
Thank you for giving me my favorite title: Momma.
You are my dreams come true.
Every word I have ever written has been for you.
Every step I have taken is to show you that you can do anything.
You will always be my greatest accomplishments.
I love you to infinity and beyond.

Mom and Dad, thank you for always supporting me. I love you.

CONTENTS

INTRODUCTION

In 2009 I was a new vice president of public policy at the New Jersey Association for the Education of Young Children (NJAEYC) attending our annual conference in Atlantic City. I kissed my children goodbye in northern New Jersey and drove down the parkway for a weekend of networking and learning. I didn't yet know that it would be the start of my work with and dedication to the concept of shared services. After days filled with keynote speakers and breakout sessions, and working the public policy table in the exhibit hall to engage participants in our Take Your Child to Vote campaign, I settled in for a closing session about the work of another AEYC (a state affiliate of the National Association for the Education of Young Children, or NAEYC) with shared services.

It was late in the day and we were all tired, but the NJAEYC board members gathered in the back of the room to learn about this new-to-us idea. NJAEYC was eager to learn new ways to engage members and offer services to early educators in our state. I hadn't heard the term *shared services* before the session, in which Sharon Easterling talked about her experience bringing shared services to her state. She described shared services as a system in which organizations come together to access material that is useful for everyone or to contract for a service that was previously not shared. Shared services, sometimes also known as *shared resources*, allows providers to pool their resources in areas where there is a common need, to better serve the children and families in their care and in turn increase the quality of care provided. Shared services is also a collaborative and evolving way to increase sustainability. Programs' success in specific areas, as well as their business overall, is increased by the engagement in shared services.

But shared services is so much more than pooling resources or providing lists and links on a website. The concept of shared services has existed in the business world since the early 2000s. The idea evolved to assist companies, especially small businesses, in saving time and money by implementing four concepts in their work:

1. Automation: using applications and other automated tools to perform work that historically has been done manually, such as calculations and other administrative work.

2. Centralization: performing similar work for multiple locations in one centralized place, such as multiple businesses coming together to use a substitute pool, access insurance, or run payroll. This is akin to how a child care center company with multiple locations operates; instead of running payroll at each location, one centralized employee runs payroll for all locations at one time.

3. Standardization: ensuring there is some uniformity or continuity in procedures and processes between locations—for example, establishing standardized procedures for collecting tuition and explaining policies to families.

4. Operations: operating the shared services unit as a business within or behind a business, almost as a core central processing unit. The operations are determined by the need of the network and happen behind the scenes of the businesses involved.

In addition to pooling resources, shared services allows businesses to seek group discounts and purchasing and to collaborate for the common good of the members in many industries. As consumers, we can see shared services at work in our everyday lives when we order from Amazon third-party sellers or merchants, book flights and trips through discount sites, and purchase gift cards from a school fundraising program.

I regularly attend professional development sessions and workshops and always enjoy learning more about the topics presented. It isn't often that a session inspires me to think about the topic in a way that could be life changing, but that is how I felt about shared services during the presentation that day. This idea, this concept, had the potential to change so many things about early childhood education and our profession. The question was—what now?

What I learned that day set me on a years-long journey of hard work to bring shared services to New Jersey and our early childhood providers. I traveled this path with Helen Muscato, my colleague at NJAEYC, and we were joined by many other shared services pioneers in our state. These collaborators included individuals from the Nicholson Foundation, the United Way of Northern New Jersey, Programs for Parents, and a number of state agencies, as well as program directors and other stakeholders from across the state. We discussed the needs of providers, the options for implementation, the opportunities available, funding, and much more. We spent many years researching shared services, learning from other states, planning how to successfully bring this opportunity to New Jersey, and finally, building the system and engaging users.

During our planning, we took a close look at the two principal parts of shared services. The first piece of the puzzle is an online collection of resources and materials offering one-stop access to providers, called a *knowledge hub*, a *shared resources portal*, an *early childhood education (ECE) platform*, an *ECE Shared Resources platform*, or a *shared resources platform*. The second piece of the puzzle is the alliance, a group of providers that engage as a collective. Providers maximize their results when they use the platform and engage in an alliance, thus using both pieces of the puzzle.

Finally, we arrived at a plan to split our system into two parts: the knowledge hub, called NJ Shared Resources, would be purchased and managed by NJAEYC, and the alliances would be researched, developed, and administered by Programs for Parents, a child care resource and referral agency (CCR&R) led by Dr. Beverly Lynn, a leader in our field who understood the need for and potential impact that alliances had for our providers. A CCR&R helps families find care and provides resources for child care businesses, such as start-up, licensing, and accreditation assistance; professional development and training; and advocacy support. The alliances would develop in pockets across the state to address the needs of providers in each region after a pilot period within Essex County where Programs for Parents is located. Together the platform and the alliances would create the woven design of New Jersey's shared services network and allow early childhood providers the best opportunity to collaborate to save time, save money, and focus efforts on building sustainable, quality early childhood programs. We would also continue to work together as a steering committee to ensure collaboration and the integration of the various pieces.

I am beyond proud of the work that we have done in New Jersey to build a collaborative system for shared services that is spreading across our state. After we began both the NJ Shared Resources platform and the alliances, we still had much work to do: educating others about the concept of shared services and the available opportunities, developing resources, establishing relationships, and building a system of shared resources across our state. The most time-consuming part of the project continues to be providing education and spreading understanding around the project and its multifaceted structure, but we are consistently growing our shared services networks across the state and increasing awareness among professionals.

Shared services in the field of early childhood education has been slowly gaining attention since 2009, beginning with the founding work of Louise Stoney and John Weiser at Opportunities Exchange. Opportunities Exchange is a nonprofit group that works to inform, educate, and support the field as it strives to provide high-quality, sustainable child care for all children. One way it does so is by working to increase the industry's understanding of shared services, including knowledge hubs and alliances. Opportunities Exchange provides resources, examples, and start-up guides for staffed family child care networks (SFCCNs), multi- and single-site centers, and other types of programs as well. An SFCCN has paid staff who provide services and resources to local family child care businesses and is an alliance structure that is designed to meet the needs of family care providers. The other shared services alliances structures operate in other ways as well.

Another instrumental force in the growth of shared services is the development of knowledge hubs through the company CCA for Social Good. CCA for Social Good manages, designs, operates, and grows shared services knowledge hubs for customers across the United States. As of 2022, not all states have existing knowledge hubs or alliances. Supporters of shared services hope to change this. Expanding alliances and knowledge hubs across the country will allow the concept of shared services in various forms to continue to grow and benefit the field.

Who Is This Book Intended For?

Shared services and the ideas and opportunities within this book will be useful to you regardless of your position in the early childhood field:

- For early childhood teachers: this book will help you understand how to engage with shared services alliances and web portals to access resources, support, training, savings, and other important benefits that will assist you in your early childhood career.

- For directors, owners, program leaders, and administrators: in addition to the items listed above, this book will also help you apply the foundational principles of shared services to run a sustainable and successful business.

- For advocates, AEYC leaders, and funders: this book will help you better understand the process of setting up and managing shared services alliances and web-based platforms to best meet the needs of your state's early childhood organizations, with the goal of improving business sustainability and the quality of care for children and families.

I am hopeful that this book will become a tool for everyone looking to learn more about shared services and to use the model in their work. I envision a future where a generation of early childhood professionals know and engage in shared services as they enter the field; where program leaders comfortably support and engage with others to streamline their efforts and increase the quality in programs statewide; and where state leaders, stakeholders, and early childhood professionals work together to create a system that is sustainable, successful, strong, and built on a foundation made sturdy by all of our hard work and collective efforts. I envision a future where we can offer accessible, quality, and affordable care to children and families that is delivered by an experienced workforce that is respectably compensated.

To reach this goal, we all must first take the time to learn about the field of early childhood education and its history, the issues we face today, and our goals for the future. I like to think that this book will help you walk the path that I have been on for many years and write your own shared resources story like the one I told above. I hope that this book does the following:

- Helps you better understand the idea of shared services and what it means for you

- Helps you identify shared services opportunities in your state and promote collaboration with others

- Helps us pave the way toward equity and sustainability for all providers

This book will help you build a foundation for understanding shared services concepts and ideas. I arranged the information in this book to help you accomplish the following goals:

1. Review the purpose and history of child care and understand how we have gotten to where we are today.

2. Discuss the ongoing issues that the field of early childhood faces.

3. Define shared services, both online hubs and alliances, and the key features, concepts, and ideas involved.

4. Analyze your program and consider how shared services concepts can help you operate a more efficient and effective business.

5. Develop a plan to implement change in your program that meets your needs.

As you read the book, I encourage you to take notes and make plans for how to implement change in your program. Designate a notebook or journal as your Shared Services Notebook where you can play with these ideas and expand upon them. I like to take notes by chapter and make to-do lists for myself and then expand these lists into categories to keep track of ideas to nurture and work through. Whatever system works for you, reading this book and taking notes is the first step in your journey.

CHAPTER 1
WHAT IS THE PURPOSE
OF CHILD CARE?

Child care. Early childhood education. Preschool. So many names to describe the many settings where our children receive learning opportunities, care, attention, and love. Child care is a business industry that has been a part of society for hundreds of years and has evolved and changed over time. The care and education we provide to children from birth through age three supports the most crucial time of brain development in a child's life, as more than one million neural connections form every second in our youngest children (Center on the Developing Child at Harvard University, n.d.). Early childhood educators live and breathe this and many other important truths about early childhood education and the impact it has on children and families. We know that the relationships we form with young children in the early years are crucial to their social-emotional development, their mental health, and their development of resiliency.

We also know that early childhood education should be full of opportunities for children to learn through play in developmentally appropriate and hands-on ways with trusted adults and peers. Early childhood is a time of exploration, problem solving, and critical thinking. A time of smiles and discovery. Of music, movement, dramatic play, literacy, books, manipulatives, and science. A time of climbing, balancing, running, jumping, building, and creating. A time to take chances, sometimes succeeding and sometimes not, while learning about disappointment, excitement, and trying again. This time is irreplaceable for our young children. But we also know that historically, and still to some extent today, the world has not viewed child care and early education as the crucial resource that it is, and many do not view early childhood through this lens.

Early Childhood Program Types

Today early childhood education is delivered in many formats:

- For-profit programs run as businesses are designed to make profits for business owners.

- Nonprofit programs are similar to for-profit programs, except a board of directors oversees operations in lieu of an owner; their nonprofit status makes them eligible for grants and other funding opportunities.

- Cooperative programs set low tuition rates, and in exchange, each enrolled family commits time to assist the program.

- Head Start, Early Head Start, and other state-funded or federally funded programs, such as those for children with special needs and military child care, are available for parents who meet the requirements for enrollment.

- College and lab schools are offered within a college or university to serve children of staff, faculty, and students and may be open to the public as well. These schools often have staff who are enrolled in teacher training programs or faculty who are dedicated to research in the early childhood field.

- Corporate centers are funded by large organizations or corporations and are operated as a benefit to the corporate employees, reducing the cost of high-quality care for employees. In some cases, families from outside the corporation are permitted to enroll to help subsidize the program.

Within these types of programs are varying modes of services. For example, a for-profit program may offer two classrooms that are state-funded and locally funded, while the other classrooms offer private care, or a nonprofit program may offer a free grant-funded summer camp.

The Truth about Child Care

The industry of early childhood education has professionalized over time, and today programs are often led by educators who are trained in early childhood education or other specialties. At the same time, early childhood leaders have attempted to grow widespread awareness regarding the truths of early childhood education and dispel myths that have long existed about the work. Some of the truths include these:

- Early childhood education is not *babysitting* or *just playing.* Children in early childhood programs are learning important foundational skills they will use for the rest of their lives, including problem solving and critical thinking. They are learning to interact with others. They are developing crucial social-emotional, language, and literacy skills while learning about relationships, community, and more.

- High-quality early childhood programs, which offer developmentally appropriate, child-centered, play-based learning, lead to positive outcomes for children and families.

- Quality relationships and interactions between caregivers and young children have a hugely positive effect on the development of children, and these relationships are a crucial part of the work of early childhood professionals.

- As it is often said in our field, play is the work of childhood. This has been demonstrated for many years; high-quality early childhood education should look as if children are playing. It is during this time that important learning is taking place.

- Early childhood teachers are worthy of the same pay and respect as other teachers.

The ideas above are just some of the advocacy topics included in this work. Yet advocating for change has been difficult, and many people within our society do not understand the importance of early childhood education. The COVID-19 pandemic brought many of the issues facing the field to the forefront of our minds and onto our television screens and social media feeds. While early childhood professionals have long known about the importance of our work as well as the issues facing the field, those outside the field were now getting a better look. The pandemic also provided a clear challenge: if child care businesses are to survive and thrive, systemic change must occur now. Shared services is a fairly new concept in the field of early education but not so new overall that we don't already have a blueprint for how to proceed.

Taking time to understand the historical context of and key developments in the field of early childhood education and child care grounds us as we look toward the future. Studying our past successes, failures, and areas of need helps us build better plans, increasing our understanding of the persistent issues that have existed and still exist in the field. Often, society at large has not grasped the scope of these issues, but today the stage is set for potential change. Whether this will actually lead to substantial change is yet to be seen. So let's move forward, but first, let's take a look back.

CHAPTER 2
LONG-STANDING ISSUES
IN THE EARLY CHILDHOOD FIELD

When we examine the issues we currently face in the early childhood field, we must acknowledge that they have their roots in the history and origins of our work. While the true beginning is difficult to pinpoint, child care can trace its origins deep in human history, as women have always helped care for one another's children. Wet nursing, caregiving, and other informal instances of child care have existed for as far back as we can look. For centuries under the systems of slavery in America, women cared for the young children of those around them. Still today, women of color earn lower wages than their white colleagues.

The first nursery school in the United States dates to 1854. In the early 1900s, social pressure still kept most married women (many of whom were mothers) from working—although within this statistic, twice as many Black married women worked than white married women. Nursery schools became more widespread in the 1930s during the Great Depression, when increasing numbers of women took jobs to support their families. The percentage of married women who were employed continued to rise through the century. Subsequently, the US government was inspired by President Lyndon Johnson's War on Poverty to begin the Head Start program in 1965, responding to low-income families' need for affordable preschool. Head Start engaged the whole child and family, offering early childhood education, family supports and engagement, and other services.

Head Start and other government-funded programs and reforms have continued over the years. Legislation such as the Child Care and Development Block Grant (CCDBG), which was passed for the first time in 1990 and was reauthorized in 2014 and 2018, and No Child Left Behind (NCLB), signed into law in 2002, improved the access, quality, and affordability of care and education for young children. The 2021 American Rescue Plan allotted $39 billion for child care relief and is hopefully a first step toward lasting funding and substantial changes for programs.

Over the years, legislation and funding have increased support for the field overall, but we also must focus specifically on increasing financial support for child care workers. Progress has been seen in small pockets over the years, with much support from NAEYC. In 2020 NAEYC and fourteen other national organizations worked together to develop a Unifying Framework, a collective vision with recommendations that seek to professionalize the workforce and unify expectations, education, worker compensation rates, and more for child care workers. We have come a long way, but there is much work to do.

Many of the issues that persist in the field stem from its roots in slavery and a workforce that has continued to be predominately female and disproportionately featuring Black, Indigenous, and people of color. In addition, early childhood education was historically not a part of the public school system, and as such it was underfunded, undersupported, and undervalued. Further, there has been little focus on unifying the profession across states and programs in terms of quality, compensation, and educator preparation, among other factors. To finally take steps forward, we must address the fundamental issues that we have been facing for years.

Child Care Workers Are Underpaid

The long-existing issue of underpayment is an obstacle to retaining professionals in the early childhood field. Traditionally, early childhood education has been a female-centric profession, contributing to the low pay of workers. In addition, society has tended to undervalue the specialized skills and training that are required of early childhood professionals. Recently, there are plentiful accounts that child care workers could work fewer hours in less stressful environments and earn more money and better overall benefits in retail and other industries. At the time of writing in 2022, you could read stories in your news feeds daily about chains like Target, supermarkets, and other big-box stores offering starting positions at $24 per hour, and companies like Starbucks paying for college tuition and offering benefits including health insurance and retirement savings plans. Even educators who have completed training programs, hold early childhood education degrees, or have substantial classroom experience can often do better financially in other fields. The Center for the Study of Child Care Employment reported in 2020 that women, and especially women of color, have long been expected to work for low wages (McLean et al. 2020). The Center for American Progress (Bleiweis, Frye, and Khattar 2021) reports that even as child care work is one of the lowest-paid professions, African American women make just eighty-four cents for every dollar that white women make in the field.

Professionals in the early childhood field are often eligible for federal or state subsidies or fall into a category defined as Asset Limited, Income Constrained, Employed (ALICE). The United Way of Northern New Jersey (n.d.) developed the acronym in 2009, building the work of United for ALICE (www.unitedforALICE.org) since then. ALICE families operate above the federal poverty level but struggle to afford a family's basic needs. In 2022 the eligibility criteria marking the federal poverty level for a family of four was $27,750 a year (HHS 2022). Families who earned above this marker did not have access to programs made available to individuals and families who live under the poverty level, and they were expected to operate their family budget on their salaries alone without assistance. This is no easy task and is in many ways impossible. When ALICE families are faced with housing costs, child care fees, and the many other expenses associated with managing a family, they simply cannot make ends meet.

Since its initial inception, the work of United for ALICE has grown, and in 2022 it was a part of the conversation and research in twenty-eight states. United for ALICE researchers bring awareness to ALICE workers and present data to support the development of programs that bring change to this problem. The ALICE Wage Tool provides data on ALICE workers and families by state (United for ALICE 2018). It allows us to better understand what ALICE workers are paid, providing data to illustrate just how serious this problem is.

In the 2020s, a vast number of child care workers are ALICEs themselves or live in ALICE households. Hundreds of thousands of child care and early education workers are employed across the United States, and the majority of them make at or near the local minimum wage (which cannot be lower than the federal minimum rate but in some states and localities is higher). As a side note here, I highly recommend you search online to find the minimum wage in your state, and compare it to other states too, to aid your understanding of this issue for child care workers, as well as all workers who make at or close to minimum wage. Hundreds of thousands of these crucial workers make less than $15 per hour and are expected to support their families—nearly impossible in society today.

We know that these hourly wages are not enough to make ends meet, support a family, or save and plan for the future, and we must advocate for change in this area. As of 2022, the federal minimum wage had not increased since 2009. While some states have recently seen minimum wage increases, there is still a long way to go to bring child care workers to parity with their public school counterparts. Indeed, many argue that our public school teachers are still underpaid, so what does that say for our early childhood workforce, who make a fraction of that salary and are not provided close to the same benefits and other supports? Many child care workers are not offered benefits, such as opportunities to plan for retirement through their jobs, and are not even eligible for the public service loan forgiveness programs that public school teachers can access. It is no wonder that professionals are leaving the field to find better opportunities elsewhere.

Shared services is not the answer to the wage crisis that is plaguing the child care field. However, shared services allows us to identify areas in child care businesses where we can save money. Engaging with shared services supports programs in building sustainable businesses and finding new ways to operate, which in turn can free up or create new resources so program leaders can pay a higher wage.

Child Care Workers Are Not Respected as Educators

Society has often viewed child care workers as babysitters who do an unskilled job or as employees who can be replaced easily, instead of the skilled and trained professionals they are. Early educators are often highly qualified and educated, with associate's and bachelor's degrees or even higher education, and not only are they poorly compensated, but they also are not respected for having these qualifications. This disparity is again rooted in the misogynistic and racist foundation that the early childhood field was built on.

Early childhood education has been ignored or seen as inferior or less important than other types of education, but in reality, early childhood (spanning birth through third grade) is the most active developmental and educational time period in a child's life. Our brains build more neural connections in the first eighteen months of life than at any other time. Early childhood educators must skillfully design the learning environment, build caring relationships, and lead the hands-on play that is the essential work of our youngest learners. I like to think of early childhood teachers as brain architects: they are building the foundation for the relationships, development, and learning that will take place throughout a child's life. It is time for society to change its views about early care workers and appreciate them as the professionals they are.

While shared services cannot solve this problem on its own, it can offer opportunities for collective advocacy efforts, provide a means to call attention to issues that need change, and usher in a collective way to approach these changes from a strong and unified front. Shared services allows members to come together and look for new solutions to old problems.

Many Early Childhood Leaders Were Teachers First

Many owners, directors, and program leaders were previously early educators themselves. They often say they became leaders in the field out of a dedication to the children and families they serve. While they are skilled educators and pedagogical leaders who implement a strong curriculum, build quality programs, and engage families with care, they may not have business skills or experience in building budgets, planning payroll, collecting tuition, and fulfilling other administrative tasks that lead to program sustainability.

Trajectory of Early Childhood Leaders

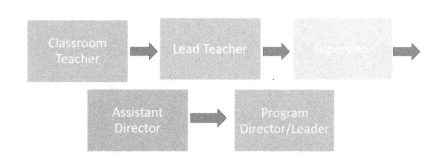

This traditional trajectory illustrates why we need to help early education program leaders build their skills in business leadership, because their programs are in fact businesses. While business management skills may not be our first or strongest skill set, they are necessary to ensure that our businesses survive and thrive. Rather than trying to change this pathway by bringing in business managers (likely lacking in early childhood skills and competencies) to lead our programs, we have the opportunity to do two things:

1. Train program leaders, who are already successful in education, to be strong business leaders.

2. Contract with outside groups to complete business tasks and collaborate with other alliance members for the benefit of all in the group. For example, if alliance members agree that processing payroll isn't a task they do well, they may decide to collectively contract with a payroll company to do this work for them.

When we view our programs as businesses, we see our "services" differently. Programs benefit from strong business practices and strategies in addition to strong educational practices. We must approach leadership with a multifaceted approach that includes training and skills in business management. The McCormick Center for Early Childhood Leadership researches the need for and implementation of effective program leadership in the early childhood field. There are more than twenty-seven times as many leadership training programs for K–12 leaders than for early childhood leaders (Talan and Magid 2021). Child care centers and early childhood programs need leadership training and programs as well. Shared services can help, both with leader training and with collective contracting of outside resources for business tasks.

Remember that the child care industry was built on the backs of women, especially Black women and other women of color, who were not always respected and or seen as businesspeople in their own right. Identifying this as a problem in the profession allows us to brainstorm ways to strengthen business skills and ultimately the field as a whole. Today, as we rebuild the field and the societal views of child care workers, we are also building the idea that early childhood leaders are strong and savvy business owners who fulfill a critical role in society.

The Funding Cycle Is Challenging

The US child care system developed to meet children's needs in response to economic changes within our society. It has grown over the years, evolving into a privately funded industry that has supports from the federal government in specific situations. For example, federal funding supports Head Start, quality rating and improvement systems (QRISs), and CCR&Rs. QRISs are designed to rate centers for quality and promote quality improvement across states. Another federal support comes through subsidy payments. If a family meets the poverty-level income requirements, they may be eligible for a government subsidy. However, the subsidy is approximately one-third the amount of tuition, leaving two-thirds to be split between a family copay and a loss to the center. When programs are already operating on a slim or nonexistent profit margin, this can be a huge problem.

Most child care businesses do not receive subsidies and are left to manage their own finances by gathering tuition and income that covers the cost of salaries, building expenses, and other financial demands, while trying to make a profit and offer quality care at the same time. This can be a difficult if not an almost impossible feat, and the system cannot sustain itself in its current state.

There are various ways that programs attempt to manage this difficult funding cycle, absent funding from the government. Nonprofit programs may be eligible for grants, but they must search for the grants, apply for them, track progress, report data, and repeat this process. This can be a great opportunity for programs that have a leader who is savvy in grant writing and grant management—but not all are. Co-ops rely on parent involvement to keep tuition and salaries low. Labs and programs associated with colleges and universities, as well as corporate centers (run by large companies for their employees), often receive support from the larger organization. For-profit and nonprofit centers often rely heavily on fundraising. I have seen many creative ways to address the fact that tuition is already high and salaries are still low. Yet managing a program is expensive and a delicate balancing act, and more and more programs are struggling daily with the fact that they cannot pay educators less but most parents cannot afford to pay more.

Time for Change

Now is the time to address these systemic issues and make meaningful changes that finally bring respect, equity, and sustainability to the field of early childhood education. Change is more necessary than ever—and it is also more attainable than ever. The stage is set as never before, with the light shining brightly on the field of early care and education. Shared services and a new outlook will serve us as we collectively work to improve the outcomes for children and families, for staff, and for child care businesses in a long-term response. We can save time and money while focusing on the quality of care we provide and the ways we provide it.

The child care field was stressed prior to COVID-19, and the massive effect of the pandemic on society as a whole and the child care industry in particular left us on the brink of collapse. Enrollment dropped as families found alternative arrangements during the pandemic. Meanwhile, workers left the field in large numbers. This may be in part due to the phenomenon of "the great resignation" that we saw nationwide as COVID-19 effects ebbed and people in every industry quit their jobs. But even if so, it is just exacerbating the long-existing problem that program leaders cannot compensate staff in a way that retains qualified workers long-term. Program leaders are now searching unsuccessfully for staff, closing classrooms, trying to balance their days between covering classrooms and doing office work, and making difficult choices, such as postponing necessary improvements or leaving bills unpaid. While some centers and programs have waiting lists because they are unable to recruit and retain staff, others are closing at a rapid rate. How can centers stay open if they can't staff their classrooms and can't pay their bills, and if the leadership is facing extreme burnout? At the same time, as centers close, families that need care find themselves living in child care deserts where access is limited or slots are full. What does a family do when their provider suddenly closes? Each of these problems adds to the already growing mountain of issues facing programs and families in the current state of care.

Learning from the Pandemic

When COVID-19 stopped our world in its tracks, a few select professions and services continued operating so that we could meet the emergency needs of the public. The first were medical professionals at hospitals, followed by the essential workers who sold food, toilet paper, and other necessary supplies. After it became apparent that the two-week shutdown would extend, employers began making long-term plans to work from home. Many of us became experts at Zoom and Microsoft Teams, creating office spaces and classrooms in our dining rooms and basements. As a single parent, I had to quickly create workspaces for myself, overtaking my kitchen table, and also for my children, that let us all concentrate but also allowed me to supervise them easily when needed. Essential workers didn't have the ability to work from home, but to return to work, they needed to find safe arrangements for their children whose schools and early childhood settings had been temporarily shut down. In response, emergency orders on a state-by-state basis called for select child care programs to remain open. This was one of the first actions that called national attention to the fact that child care workers are crucial, essential workers. Without child care programs, our economy grinds to a literal stop.

With this return to business, programs faced new questions. Programs were open again, which was a positive step, but they were operating under emergency guidelines that limited attendance to emergency workers' children only and limited the number of children in each classroom and center, so programs had significantly less revenue. Staff operated under specific limitations surrounding classroom assignments, materials used, food served, and health and safety procedures. Programs struggled to remain open, pay the rent or mortgage, and cover the salaries of workers when they also had to negotiate the high cost of personal protective equipment (PPE) and all manner of supplies (which now had to be assigned to each child so that there was no cross-contamination), while serving only a few children at a time, adding additional office work each day, overseeing food and outdoor safety, tracking attendance and health questionnaires, storing items according to emergency guidelines, and more. The field that was stressed before COVID-19 was at a breaking point.

Shared services offered some solutions to programs as they pooled resources to offer low-cost cleaning supplies and PPE. Programs also pooled together to create templates for COVID-19 policies. Some other solutions were these:

- Emergency federal funding for child care centers to cover critical needs such as salaries

- State-level executive orders to provide PPE and support other program needs

- Grants for PPE and cleaning supplies, as well as other small-business grants and loan programs

- Donations from individuals and nonprofit organizations, including PPE, extra blankets to meet COVID-19 licensing guidelines in infant and toddler rooms, bins to store children's belongings safely, and additional toys and art materials so each child could have their own materials instead of sharing them

Where Do We Go from Here?

While temporary initiatives and supports were helpful to businesses during the pandemic, the question remained: What would happen after things returned to "normal"? Centers and family child care homes were closing every day. Could the field weather the storm? Hiring and retaining staff was always difficult, but the new requirements and additional pressure made it even more challenging. The cost families bear doesn't produce the funds needed to provide quality care, and subsidy payments cover only a fraction of tuition. What "normal" did we want to return to?

Yet we had waited years for the advocacy efforts and dedicated attention that the field was finally beginning to receive. We have heard our story a million times before—but many others were seeing child care workers in a new light and hearing about these problems for the first time. They were seeing their family's child care workers as essential to their family, their jobs, and the economy. The issues were being discussed on national television by our president, on our social media feeds, and in conversations across the nation.

The public, families, politicians, and others were finally beginning to understand that child care also drives our economy. One day many years ago at a NAEYC Public Policy Forum, a seasoned advocate told the group that if we want our politicians to understand child care, we can't just talk about the benefits of quality care; we have to present the issues clearly in terms of dollars, business, and economic success. Child care is not just a child issue but a national issue. Without affordable, accessible quality care for their children, families cannot go to work, businesses cannot stay open, and our economy cannot thrive. Moreover, while our children are in care, they are engaged in early childhood education that will support their social-emotional, cognitive, physical, and language development. They create and become problem solvers and critical thinkers, the innovators of tomorrow.

For early childhood programs to succeed and thrive, we must address the historical issues and barriers, and we must also implement successful educational and business practices within programs. Programs must offer a strong early education curriculum delivered by qualified and engaged staff and led by a leadership team that understands that while educational quality is crucial, strong business management skills ensure the program can keep providing quality care.

Now is the time to call attention to and focus on shared services in the field of early childhood care and education so that we can build a system that is sustainable for now and for the future. While we need increased attention, funding, resources, and supports from government sources, shared services provides a way for early childhood professionals to push positive change now. Using shared services models allows programs to support children, families, and the workforce toward the goal of building a sustainable system overall.

CHAPTER 3
CONNECTING THE DOTS: KNOWLEDGE HUBS

The first component of shared services is the knowledge hub. A shared services knowledge hub is a web-based service through which users access online resources. These web portals may be familiar to you, but if not, this is a great time to explore the opportunities available in your state. A knowledge hub also may be referred to as a *shared resources platform* or simply by a formal name given by the organization that runs it.

Utilizing shared resources knowledge hubs is a great way for educators to avoid wasting time re-creating the wheel. For example, if you are developing a parent handbook, you do not need to create a handbook from scratch when you can download a template from the knowledge hub and customize it to meet your program's needs. Whether you are a program director creating a marketing or crisis management plan or a teacher looking for templates for your next parent-teacher conference, knowledge hubs can provide resources that will help you save time in your work each day.

CCA for Social Good started and operates the ECE Shared Resources platforms that exist across the country. In 2022 it partnered with thirty-four states and the District of Columbia to operate knowledge hubs. CCA for Social Good allows only one hub per state. Each knowledge hub is owned by an organization or group of organizations in each state. Organizations pay CCA for Social Good an initial development fee and then a yearly licensing fee to own and operate their site. Two versions of sites are available: a custom site and a standard version (ECE Shared Resources, n.d.). The custom site allows owners to add content of their own in addition to the content created by CCA for Social Good. Some hubs are free to everyone, but some have paid access only. Some come as a benefit of belonging to a larger membership organization, such as a state AEYC. You can visit www.ecesharedresources.com /working-with-us/partners-impact (top QR code) or www.oppex.org (bottom QR code) to see if a platform is currently operating in your state. You can also reach out to CCA for Social Good to find out. If there is a platform, they can connect you with those in charge to help you set up an account. If there isn't, this is a great

opportunity to ask whether conversations with interested organizations in your state are happening and, if not, to consider how to spark these conversations and bring the platform to your state.

Currently, sites are owned and operated by the following:

- State AEYCs

- CCR&Rs

- Other organizations, foundations, and nonprofits

- Collaborative groups of the organizations mentioned above

Some knowledge hubs have evolved into large operations that work daily to engage users in the collaborative aspects of shared services. Once you locate the shared services platform in your state, you can learn more about who operates the hub, what resources are available, and how access is granted.

How to Start a Shared Resources Platform

1. If no platform exists in your state, reach out to CCA for Social Good to inquire whether conversations have been started with stakeholders in your state.

2. If conversations have started, CCA for Social Good staff may be able to connect you to the conversations. If not, you can meet with the staff to discuss the different knowledge hub opportunities available. They will also be able to suggest ideas for funding and provide other start-up help.

3. Become familiar with other platforms and the groups that manage them. CCA for Social Good may also be able to connect you to platform owners in other states that are similar to your group, such as an AEYC team, a state government team, a nonprofit team, or another organization.

4. Enter the planning phase to start determining where to go from here.

What Can the Knowledge Hub Do?

Each knowledge hub has the same basic information. If a state has a custom site, it also offers state-specific information and additional content. For example, each standard site includes a family child care toolkit. In New Jersey, NJAEYC owns a custom site and has added information to the toolkit, such as training links provided by our state agencies, local opportunities for professional development, necessary and relevant resources, and other important information.

Custom Content in New Jersey

In my own state of New Jersey, our custom site allows us to provide information that is specific to our state. Since our platform is owned and operated by NJAEYC, the state AEYC affiliate, we have NAEYC- and NJAEYC-specific information. Other resources that are pertinent to providers and professionals across the state include the following:

- Resources from Grow NJ Kids, our state QRIS

- COVID-19 resources specific to New Jersey, in addition to the COVID-19 resources updated by CCA for Social Good

- Specific information developed by the state for family child care providers; in addition, a basic family child care toolkit from CCA for Social Good that New Jersey has customized

- Information on state grants, funding, and other financial opportunities

- State and local training opportunities

- New Jersey advocacy information

- An infant and toddler toolkit that NJAYEC created using a grant, which provides specific resources for infant and toddler professionals in the state

- New Jersey–specific training opportunities

- More evolving information that is added regularly

A custom site's resources fall under four main categories:

1. Engaging families: resources to increase family engagement within your program, including newsletters, conference templates, conversation guides, communication resources, and more.

2. Running the classroom: resources to help with curriculum, classroom management, and many other aspects of daily classroom work.

3. Saving money: resources to access insurance, teacher discount programs, and other ways to save.

4. Managing programs: resources to tackle administration and management tasks efficiently, such as templates, forms, links, documents, and other materials.

Resources in each category include templates, articles, ideas, forms, policies, and other items that are useful to teachers, assistants, administrators, and other early education professionals. For just one example, some platform owners, including New Jersey, feature an early childhood education jobs service that allows members to post jobs to multiple platforms (such as Indeed, CareerBuilder, and similar sites) while paying for the listing just once, realizing a tremendous savings. Saving time and money with the resources on the site allows educators to reinvest those resources to increase the quality of care and education for children and families.

Some of the most important offerings on the shared resources hubs are resources that guide program leaders in building stronger business practices. These resources can be found throughout the four categories on the hub platforms. The training, resources, templates, and support for various aspects of business management can include materials on these topics:

- Recruiting and retaining staff: templates and resources ranging from adaptable job postings and interview questions to retention plans, dental and vision plans, and other benefits.

- Marketing: marketing plans, resources for creating a website, templates for advertising, and other tips and tricks.

- Business and strategic planning: business plan and strategic plan templates, suggestions for mission and vision statements, adaptable crisis management and risk management plans, support for creating presentations for board meetings, and more.

- Tax planning and preparation: budgeting forms and tax preparation forms, as well as help finding specific resources, such as Tom Copeland's articles on the Time-Space Percentage.

- Human resources practices: adaptable scripts for having difficult conversations, termination forms, employee recognition ideas, templates for improvement plans, and more.

If you are not yet a user of a shared resources platform, look up the organization that holds the license in your state and sign up to become a user today. Using the site as an integral part of your operations is an opportunity to redesign your day and your work and to reinvest this time in other areas of your business. As I mentioned above, if you are not sure if your state has an operating knowledge hub, reach out to someone at CCA for Social Good to find out, and ask for help in joining or starting a conversation about bringing a platform to your state. You can even reach out to me, and I can provide some guidance in starting this conversation. In the meantime, visit the Opportunities Exchange website to learn more about the shared services concepts from the experts there.

CHAPTER 4
WORKING TOGETHER:
SHARED SERVICES ALLIANCES

The second component of shared resources is an alliance. A shared services alliance is a small group of child care providers who join together to address the complex business and professional problems they face. The goal of an alliance is to pool resources to work more efficiently and effectively, often through collaboration with other program leaders. Shared services alliances can consist of child care centers of various types as well as family child care providers. The alliance members function as a team with a core or hub that centralizes jobs or tasks that members of the alliance agree to share, such as bulk purchasing, engaging legal services in retainment for the group, creating a substitute pool, running payroll, and more. Alliances can be visualized as a wheel, with a hub (the alliance or business center) and spokes (the small-business entities organized around the hub).

Opportunities Exchange reported that as of 2022, over twenty-one states were home to at least one shared services alliance (Opportunities Exchange, n.d.). There are likely many alliance-type programs being piloted across the country that are not included in this statistic.

Some of the many alliances across the country were founded in conjunction with the state's knowledge hub, and some are separate entities. Some states do not have active alliances, some have one, and some have multiple alliances. Different alliances function differently:

- They have been in operation for varying time periods.

- They have different funding sources.

- They serve different populations.

- They offer different services.

- They have varying costs to join.

Yet alliances across locations have core similarities:

- Alliances are local networks that address the needs of enrolled programs. The needs of one alliance look different from the needs of another, but there are some similarities across alliances and lessons we can learn from groups that have been operating for a long time.

- Alliances may serve a specific group of providers, such as infant-toddler programs or family child care programs, or they may be broader in their scope and serve, for example, child care centers generally. Alliances offer opportunities, trainings, and other resources tailored to meet the needs of the group. Needs are determined by detailed and timely needs analyses.

- One key factor that should be encouraged by alliances is automation systems. (Read more about automation systems in chapter 6.)

Just as the organization and makeup of alliances vary, the work of alliances varies as well. Regardless of the specific work of an alliance, the outcome should be that members share a benefit and are operating in a new way that allows them to be more efficient, using collaborative methods that are meaningful to all members. If an alliance is accessing a substitute pool or engaging in strategies for strengthening business practices, the goal should be for everyone to benefit from the tools, which have been developed out of a needs assessment and at a prompting of the members of the alliance. Many alliances offer financial and business management services or require members to adopt a data management and business accounting tool. However, they may offer resources and support in many other areas, some of which are discussed below:

- Substitute and staffing services: including marketing, interviewing, hiring, onboarding, and retention support for substitute and permanent staff, and a pool of substitutes available to all alliance members.

- Training, professional development, and coaching: including virtual or in-person opportunities and ranging from stand-alone trainings to expanded sessions that involve multiple forms of training on a range of topics.

- Accounting and financial services: such as payroll services, program accounting, bookkeeping, and automation.

- Classroom assessment services: for example, collaborating to hire someone to evaluate classroom environments or student progress and learning goals.

- Child assessment training and support: programs can also collaborate in ways that will help them save time in administering and evaluating assessments.

- Quality improvement, certification, and licensing support: accreditation and QRIS navigation can be a time-consuming process, and support from a central party can help save time and ensure that programs navigate the processes efficiently while the regular staff continues to work on their regular assignments.

- Bulk purchasing to realize savings on food and paper products, uniforms, supplies, cleaning, and other services.

Shared services alliances provide a transformational opportunity for programs to operate more efficiently and to move toward sustainability. As early childhood professionals looking to the future of our businesses and our industry, we must be open to a complete overhaul of the way things *have been* done to imagine the way things *can* be done. We need to see this opportunity not as a threat but as a pathway to success, not as a negative statement about the way we have been doing things, but rather as a newly born way for us to be a part of the future. For example, if you haven't been examining rates and enrollment to maximize revenue, now is the time to start. If you don't have policies and procedures for onboarding new employees, that is okay, but now is the time to develop them so that you can provide staffing experiences that benefit both your business and employees. Shared services alliances can help you identify areas for needed change and provide the collaboration and support you need to make the changes.

Preparing to Join an Alliance

- Reading up on existing alliances is a great place to start. Try beginning with the Opportunities Exchange website. You can learn from what is working for other alliances even if their work and goals are not specifically relevant in your situation. How did they come to offer these services? Are you overlooking any aspects of your business? What can you learn from less successful attempts that other alliances have made?

- I also recommend that you reflect on any experiences in your career that relate to the idea of alliances. I think back to my early days as a child care center director. I was fresh out of college and found myself operating and managing a new child care program, and I joined a local directors group at the recommendation of my local CCR&R. I was shy, quiet, eager, and had a lot to learn. I remember attending well-organized meetings that offered professional development in areas carefully chosen to help me and the other attendees. I got to know others in similar positions to me, shared ideas and stories, and built relationships. I learned about what was required as well as what additional work and ideas others were putting into their programs. I often think of this experience as a very early and simple version of an alliance, and it helps me see the benefits of engaging in programs where I can collaborate and learn with others.

- If there are no shared services alliances in your state, using the Opportunities Exchange website to gather information and then engaging with local stakeholders is a great way to start the conversation. It may take some brainstorming to determine where to begin your work. For example, in New Jersey, the first road to shared services started with our AEYC. Once the AEYC was on board, we formed a stakeholders committee that included representation from CCR&Rs, the state offices, and a private foundation that offered funding support.

How Alliances Are Formed

An alliance is usually formed by an agency or group of agencies, sometimes working with other individuals or entities that provide visibility or funding. For example, in New Jersey, a number of shared services–based alliances have developed out of private funding, state funding, philanthropic dollars, and other stakeholders' contributions.

Often, shared services alliances are initially funded by donor and grant dollars, but over the years they develop plans for sustainability. Funders like the Kellogg Foundation and similar national organizations have an interest in developing sustainable and high-quality systems for early childhood education. Many state and local funders and organizations also support the idea of shared services. They recognize that child care is a crucial building block for the success of communities, the economy, and the American family.

In my experience, developing a plan to build shared services opportunities can take years. NJAEYC first discussed the concept at a conference and then as part of a joint team with Programs for Parents (a CCR&R) and a private foundation that would provide funding to launch the venture. Ultimately our plan included a two-pronged approach: NJAEYC took the lead on the platform and Programs for Parents would lead the alliance. Each entity would build a foundation for the future of each branch but ensure that they also linked the two together for maximum benefits. Regardless of what your potential plan is, make sure you take the time necessary during this phase to design and build the programs you want.

Forming the Group

Once the planning stages are over, the next step is establishing the group. This doesn't necessarily mean engaging members immediately. The team may spend months or years just building the infrastructure of the group. This includes determining the alliance's staffing needs and job descriptions, hiring the staff, setting up procedures for the alliance, and understanding the processes that will occur once members are engaged.

Next, the alliance can begin to onboard members and start the process of establishing relationships between providers. This relationship building is one of the most important steps for a new alliance, and it should focus on these goals:

- Listening

- Sharing

- Being open to ideas and change

- Establishing trust

Building relationships is critical because for child care providers, working collaboratively with other programs likely isn't instinctive. We often see other programs as competition and maybe even hold our program information secretly, operating on our own without support and collaboration. A new alliance team may spend weeks and months getting to know one another. Your first meetings may consist of activities designed to engage one another, to get to know one another, and to build trust and communication within the group so that everyone can share openly and freely.

Developing Goals and Identifying the Work of the Alliance

The goals of the alliance may already be well established, or they may still be developing. If you are joining an established alliance at your local CCR&R, they may have set goals already. If an alliance is just starting, you may be a part of developing the goals together. The goals of an alliance may be related to program and system-wide opportunities for success, such as these:

- Increasing program sustainability by building business practices

- Addressing a staffing issue that is present across the area

- Engaging providers to identify areas in which they could operate more efficiently

While working to establish trust and positive relationships, and keeping the goals of the alliance in mind, alliance leaders and members are also gathering information on everyone's needs, including those related to human resources, business and financial management, food service, licensing and registration, health and safety, quality improvement, curricula, and technology. Another key role of alliances is building members' confidence and experience as strong and competent business owners.

Examining the needs, strengths, and weaknesses of the providers is important because these shared needs will steer the alliance's priorities and determine what types of resources it will focus on. Gathering this information may happen through surveys, informal conversations, or a more formal review of the current practices in each program. If the alliance finds that most or all programs need payroll services, automation systems, and substitute pools, the alliance's work will likely include researching opportunities in these areas and eventually providing these services. Identifying these items is an important step, but it is also ongoing work, as priorities need to be discussed, revised, and managed as conditions change.

My Alliance Story

I have worked as a team member on six different shared services projects to date. The first few months of my work with new shared services groups usually includes getting to know one another and establishing relationships, strategies, assessment tools, and infrastructure. The small-business owners who join are often women, and while the concept of shared services is mostly new to them, they usually join with an open mind and desire to grow. Exploring the vision and goals of each business and getting to know one another as colleagues and individuals to build trust was crucial to success for all. This step is perhaps the most important, as building trust among alliance members and the shared services team opens the door to collaboration and change, turning us into colleagues who can rely on one another when we are in need, want to collaborate, or have information and ideas to share. This relationship building isn't a one-time job but an ongoing part of our work. Needs assessments are ongoing during this time.

While many providers communicate their need for technical support in multiple areas, business management is often at the top of each of their lists. Providers want to work on their curriculum and quality, but they needed to get the business side of their work sorted out to do so effectively. I recommend breaking down the large category of business administration into smaller topics, such as human resources, tuition management and collection, contracts, and so on. In my experience, alliances consider the areas in which each member is strong and the areas in which they want to realize improvements or better outcomes, knowing that this is an ongoing discussion as these things change over time. Finding commonalities allows the alliance to grow and find focus.

After discussing the web-based knowledge hubs that operate in many states and examining the rise of alliances across the country, we have a well-rounded picture of how shared services operates in our field today. Shared services works most effectively when providers access and use both the knowledge hub in their state and the alliance opportunities together. Let us next dig deeper into more of the specific possibilities that shared services can offer.

CHAPTER 5
THE FOUNDATION:
THE IRON TRIANGLE

The business of child care rests on a foundation of three critical supports, which we refer to as *the iron triangle*. Louise Stoney, a founding member of Opportunities Exchange, coined the concept (Stoney 2010). When providers work to incorporate the three crucial aspects of the triangle in their business, they are building a strong foundation for their partners. Program leaders should start with the iron triangle when evaluating their program and implementing changes to make it stronger and more sustainable. Understanding each pillar and what it means for a program is an important step for every child care program as its leaders reimagine their business for success and sustainability. Implementing the iron triangle is the tip of the shared services iceberg, but its three pillars provide programs with their best chance for business success.

Once you have a solid understanding of the iron triangle principles in your business, you can make decisions and take steps to increase income, decrease expenses, better manage your business, and so on. All of these goals can be made more accessible and simple through shared resources. Remember, the desired outcome is to grow a financially successful business, save time, save money, and increase quality for children and families.

The Iron Triangle of Early Childhood Programs

Full Enrollment

Understanding your enrollment and knowing how operating at full enrollment affects your bottom line are crucial to program success. Do you know what your financial picture looks like at full enrollment versus when you are operating a room that is partially enrolled? Do you know how each scenario impacts your revenue streams? Program leaders need to understand these numbers and arrange their rooms and enrolled families to maximize enrollment in each classroom. Program leaders need to know the following:

- What will you define as full enrollment? Is full enrollment for you 100 percent? Will you consider your program fully enrolled at 85 to 95 percent, which is perhaps a more achievable number that still allows for success? Whatever percentage the leadership team chooses should be used to calculate other necessary parts of the formula.

- What is the total enrollment of a program? Each classroom? What is the actual daily and weekly enrollment? How does this compare to the total licensed capacity?

- If you have an indoor playroom in your program space, how does this affect your capacity? Does it change your licensed capacity? How does it affect quality and your bottom line?

- Look at the total number of unenrolled spots and consider why these spots might be unenrolled. This may lead to questions and conversations about part-time care, vacations, and other flexible scheduling options. It may also bring about larger questions about demand in the area that you serve, the success of paid advertising versus word-of-mouth advertising, and other factors that influence enrollment.

- Can you fill unenrolled slots with children who attend part-time? Or, conversely, is the fact that you take part-time students causing a problem? Can you structure your part-time slots to ensure that they add up to full-time spots?

- Do you have a waiting list for one age group but are underenrolled for another? Can you make changes here to better fill program slots?

- Consider the realistic use of your space: for example, if you have an infant room that has a licensed capacity of eleven, but you will only ever serve eight infants in this space, you must work this into your business formulas.

Part-Time Care

Part-time care includes children who attend part-time days (half or partial days) as well as children who attend fewer than five days per week. Allowing part-time enrollment is convenient for families but can cause issues for the business, as operating at full capacity is a key factor to success. If you have a child enrolled three days a week, you are holding an empty spot on the two days a week that they aren't there unless you can find a matching family that needs care for only two days per week. Some centers address the issue in these ways:

• Charging full-time rates regardless of how many days a child attends

• Charging proportionally more for part-time slots than full-time slots to discourage families from choosing them

• Not offering part-time schedules

• Dictating part-time plans that together create a full-time schedule

If you are not using a full-time equivalency (FTE) system to track enrollment for your program, including within any individual classrooms, now is the time to begin doing so. An FTE system allows you to calculate your enrollment on one scale regardless of enrollment schedule. Children who are enrolled full-time (all day, every day) are represented as 1.0. Children with part-time schedules are represented as a portion of this whole number. For example, a child enrolled for five half days would be represented as 0.5.

Once you have set your enrollment goal, you can evaluate your current situation for areas where change is possible to help meet that goal. Can you combine classrooms to make mixed-age groups and even out waiting lists for certain classrooms? Do currently enrolled families or families in your community need a service that you could offer to help you set your program apart from others? For example, is weekend, after-school, or evening care in high demand but no one offers it? Can you redesign your marketing plan? Do you have a referral program? I encourage you to consider all options, even ones that you think are out of reach or out of the scope of your current business plan.

Full Fee Collection

Collecting all fees is the second part of the triangle. I have seen that leaders often do not visualize how significantly uncollected fees can affect the bottom line until it is in front of them in dollar form. Uncollected fees can include the following:

- Tuition that is not collected or accurately logged

- Uncollected copays from families who receive a subsidy or scholarship

- Uncollected late-payment fees

- Uncollected late-pickup fees

Why do fees go uncollected? Sometimes a program doesn't have an efficient way to manage them. Automation via shared resources can aid this process. We will discuss automation in more detail in chapter 6. When we automate contracts, billing, and fee collection, it makes the process less personal and more professional, and uncollected fees drop significantly.

As educators, we often lead with our hearts and don't charge late or excess fees when we have personal conversations with people in the collection process. This may be a reasonable business choice from time to time, but when it happens as common practice, it leads to unclear boundaries and expectations for all parties as well as a significant gap in income. Some things to consider are these questions:

- Do you have a contract that clearly states all fees, including the policies and procedures for how they will be assessed and paid?

- Do you have a rate sheet that clearly states regular fees by day and time?

- Do you implement a registration fee? Is it assessed per child or family? Is it assessed once or annually? Are these procedures clearly stated?

- Do you collect a security deposit? Are the procedures around collection and assessment clear?

- Do you have a stated fee for late pickup and late payments? Do you have a stated policy for how these fees are assessed and collected? Do you uniformly implement these policies?

- Do you have a stated policy for child sick days, snow days, school closing days, and other similar situations?

Stating these policies clearly and implementing them consistently will help eliminate issues before they arise. The best way to avoid problems with fee collection is to have clear and direct policies stating your regulations from the beginning of your relationship with families. If you don't have these things now, don't worry! Develop a clear set of policies regarding these items and identify a time (such as the beginning of a new school year, the new year in January, the beginning of summer camp, and so forth) that your new policies will take effect.

Revenue Covers the Cost per Child

Ensuring that revenue covers the cost per child is the third part of the triangle. After we set full enrollment as a goal and ensure that fees are not left uncollected, we then must cover the cost per child with our revenue. This idea is complicated by the fact that there is a ceiling on what programs can charge for care and education. Can we arrive at a number that will allow us to meet all our commitments, pay staff a respectable wage, and provide quality care, and then charge families that rate for care? Likely not. What are already considered high rates for care would skyrocket, and care would become even more unaffordable to families. There is a limit to what programs can charge.

Regardless of these limits, leaders still must run the business. You must understand exactly how much it costs you to provide care, on a very granular level. Do you know how much it costs you to operate each classroom?

- If you have two full-time and two part-time staff in your infant room, do the rates per child in that class cover salaries?

- Have you included food in the cost per child? Diapers? Have you considered costs that are part of your regular ordering as well as classroom materials and expenses that are more infrequent purchases?

- What center-wide expenses, such as automation software, utilities, and so on, are apportioned to this classroom?

After you plot out the expenses for this classroom, and every classroom, analyze your numbers based on the tuition paid for each child enrolled. Then consider the licensed capacity of the classroom. Does tuition cover the cost of the care you are providing?

If you do not understand the breakdown of costs for each classroom, stop now and do the work to better understand this concept. You can use templates on your state's ECE Shared Services platform and do an internet search for other information on this topic, but I highly recommend not skipping this step of the triangle, as it is so crucial to understanding the operations of your business.

Depending on where you are in the process of understanding your revenue and your cost per child, you may look to implement a rate increase. In my recent shared services work, my team of providers and I did a baseline evaluation of rates and then used the iron triangle to analyze each program's situation. After this lengthy and involved analysis, each provider worked out a rate increase that would help them progress toward financial stability.

I encourage you to commit to taking an honest look at your program to identify what is working and to find ways to reimagine what is not. If you have not yet examined your program in regard to the iron triangle, do it now before you move on to the other collaborative opportunities described in this book (see appendix A). Ensuring that we don't leave any money or resources on the table is a big job!

CHAPTER 6
STREAMLINING WORK: AUTOMATION

Automation through the use of a child care management system (CCMS) should be a goal of any shared services effort for child care programs, regardless of type or size. Automation allows programs to streamline the activities they must do well to keep the business side of their operation running smoothly to save time and money. Many automation programs and companies exist, and I recommend researching as many as possible when choosing one for yourself or your alliance. I also recommend using the same program across alliance members for larger bulk-use discounts, more streamlined training and troubleshooting, and easier data gathering and presenting.

Child Care Management Systems (CCMS)

A CCMS is a tool that allows programs to automate work, including billing and invoicing, child check-in and checkout, and staff schedules. Some programs that offer CCMS services include:

• Procare

• KidKare

• Brightwheel

• Tadpoles

There are several levels of engagement with automation:

- Providers locate and use automation systems to manage their programs themselves.

- The alliance offers individual providers connections to an automation system they can use in-house.

- Providers work through an alliance to contract with outside vendors to do specific pieces of operations.

- The alliance offers services to members from its centralized office. Instead of individual programs tracking their own food program data, for example, an alliance staff member performs this task for alliance members.

Examples of Automation Applications

- Family and staff data management

- Tuition tracking

- Accounts management; tracking income and expenses

- Marketing and managing leads regarding potential families, waiting lists, and so forth

- Food program and subsidy tracking

- Parent engagement; for example, by replacing the typical paper report sent home each day and instead sending information about the day, including photos and so on, electronically and automatically

- Curriculum and milestone tracking

- Website and social media management

- Professional development and training

Some program leaders will want to manage all or most automated tasks personally or with in-house staff, while others are comfortable eliminating parts of their work as much as possible to focus solely on pedagogical and other quality-improvement efforts. Programs have different needs, and leaders have different methods of approaching business, so there is no one right answer for everyone. Comfort with technology, business administration, and other related tasks may influence these decisions. Regardless, automation is a crucial part of shared services, and all providers should engage with it in some way to realize its overall savings.

Barriers to Automation and Technology Use

In my work with shared resources, I have observed that providers come to their work with varying levels of comfort surrounding technology, from home-based providers who are running their businesses with paper-and-pencil records to others who are managing their businesses completely on their phones, to directors with prior experience in business management and software operations who have a much better foundational understanding of technology. Using technology to streamline and automate the business is an important step to becoming more efficient, so it is worth investing the time to understand where providers are entering the arena and what can be done to increase their comfort levels as needed—as well as understanding your own hesitancies. As a shared resources leader, I know that understanding and communicating the importance of automation is important, but I also must understand the barriers and struggles that providers are facing in implementing automation. Careful, respectful support is necessary when barriers exist so that providers approach the process in the most positive way possible and understand the benefits as well as challenges they may face along the way. Below are some possible solutions to common barriers to using automation and other technology.

Lack of Experience or Familiarity

Being asked to engage with a new device or application can be intimidating if you do not have a lot of experience with technology. Shared services leaders should offer initial and ongoing training with devices and applications to remove this barrier. Even experienced users can benefit from brush-up courses and learn new information. When contracting with application companies, be sure that technical support and training are included.

While working with family child care providers in shared services settings, I realized early on during weekly Zoom calls that many of our home providers were operating their businesses and participating in our alliance work using only their phones. The shared services team purchased laptops and printers for each provider to support them in their business operations. After we offered initial training in Microsoft Office for all providers, we made several observations. First, we found that our alliance members were more likely to engage in training with the team because they had already established relationships with one another. We realized that individuals might not have signed up for a class on Microsoft Office on their own, but when we offered training in a group setting, they chose to attend and then requested more training together. Second, we found that even after this training, some providers were hesitant to use their computers regularly due to a lack of experience. Prioritizing time for alliance staff to connect with members and understand their concerns, worries, and fears surrounding the new devices was crucial. Even technology use boils down to relationships!

Cost and Lack of Access to Technology

Accessing and paying for technology is a real barrier for providers. In addition to the cost of the devices and software, many providers still lack reliable, affordable high-speed internet access. An alliance can help by researching grants and other funding options for technology use, or it can provide devices and access to other resources for members when they join.

Not Knowing Where to Start

Sometimes even when providers know they should use technology or an automation application, they just don't know where to start. An alliance can set up product demonstrations and walk through various automation options. Encouraging or requiring providers to use the same tools will help us professionalize our field and make progress toward data-driven outcomes.

Language Obstacles

Conferences and workshops are often presented in English and Spanish, but even when a fully dual-language experience is offered, there are often issues with the translation or implementation. Over the past few months, I have seen applications that don't offer a Spanish version or provide user support in Spanish. I have seen courses that are not offered in Spanish and English and even some that were advertised as being offered in Spanish that hadn't translated the presentation slides.

While we most often talk about English and Spanish accessibility, we must also do a better job at meeting the needs of people in the field who speak other languages. We talk in diversity workshops about ensuring that children see and hear adults leading their classes that look and sound like them. It is also our job then to ensure that we are meeting the needs of these early care professionals and engaging them in ways that are meaningful to them. While there have been and continue to be improvements, there is still a long way to go.

Not Knowing What Is Possible

Sometimes we just don't know that there are other methods, applications, or services that would allow us to do something in a more efficient and effective manner. Sharing ideas with others, learning from others' work, and investigating new products are great ways to see what is out there. An alliance group I worked with had only two family child care providers out of thirteen that understood and were using data management and automation tools when our group formed. When the others learned about these tools, they jumped at the opportunity to become involved. They still had to learn how to best use the tools, but knowing of their existence was a big step in the right direction.

The bottom line remains that technology and automation are crucial to efficiency and success, and an alliance team can offer valuable support. In the work I am doing with a shared services–based network, we understand that technology and automation are priorities, and we learn new lessons every day about our members' technology needs and barriers.

Not Tech Savvy? Use This Top Five List to Improve Your Skills

1. Check out tech schools, local community colleges, or community nonprofits for classes or trainings on technology.

2. Reach out to your local CCR&R for any trainings they may offer or be able to connect you to.

3. Do you have a shared services platform in your state? If so, ask them about available trainings.

4. Enlist fellow early childhood professionals to work together to grow your skills in areas of technology where you need support.

5. Practice, practice, practice!

CHAPTER 7
LEVERAGING SHARED SERVICES

We have a finite amount of time in our days, and as program leaders and early childhood educators, we are often juggling many tasks. Do you currently spend time updating policies and paperwork for your program? Maybe this could be completed more efficiently through a shared services resource, where you could access policy templates and other forms. If you were not creating these documents from scratch, you could have more time to observe classrooms or engage in reflective supervision with your staff. Think about how different your days could be if you took advantage of more shared services.

When I speak to people about saving time by using shared resources, I like to call attention to all of the work they do and how time savings could be realized by using materials that already exist. When I was a director, I would make myself to-do lists each week. I spent a good part of my days ensuring that paperwork and other required center information was accurate and complete. I would work through the licensing requirements, and when we were participating in our state QRIS, I would work through the required items for this system as well. I ensured that our parent handbook had the required information, updated policies, created new marketing materials, and evaluated staff. All of this is important and necessary work to ensure that a center is operating appropriately, but it is also work that takes a significant amount of time. After becoming a user of shared services, I created my to-do lists with a different lens. If I was creating a new policy, I could go to the knowledge hub to download a template. If I need a report about tuition, I could go to my automation software to download the form instead of creating and inputting it myself. If I needed to purchase supplies, I used the bulk purchasing option or sought out discounts on the website.

Preliminary Research and Assessment

Saving time and money are interchangeable and interrelated. Identifying ways in which you can save both will help your overall business performance and let you focus more on other areas that are important to your program. As you assess your current practices and identify areas for potential change or savings, take a deep look at what is currently happening in your business. Questions you may want to ask include these:

1. Am I effectively and efficiently engaging in family communication? Do I ensure that current families are engaged and happy with services provided?

2. Do I have clear enrollment procedures?

3. Can I implement more efficient human resources practices or contract this service out?

4. Do I have an effective marketing plan?

5. Do I need support in classroom management, curriculum implementation, or assessment?

6. Are licensing and other quality-measuring tasks taking too much of my time?

7. Am I tracking tuition owed and tuition paid?

8. Do I have a budget? Do I keep income and expense records?

9. Do my business records allow me to identify areas for improvement?

10. In which areas of my business would I like to save money? Have I searched for money-saving opportunities?

11. In which areas would I like to delegate or share tasks to save myself time?

12. What areas of leadership and program management would I like to focus on more, such as leading with reflective supervision, understanding adverse childhood experiences (ACEs), implementing developmentally appropriate practices, or any other topic? Maybe you'd like to develop a family engagement plan and calendar or join in more community-based events. These are items that can make it onto your to-do list with the extra time saved from other tasks.

Once you have performed a basic assessment of the business, begin a list of the tasks that are taking a lot of your time and a list of areas you feel would benefit from additional attention, and then start brainstorming ways to reimagine the time-consuming tasks so you can redirect your time and energy. I have included a worksheet in appendix B for you to use for these purposes.

Be sure to look for existing resources and opportunities that you are not taking advantage of yet:

1. Visit your local ECE Shared Resources platform. If you do not have an account, see how you can become a member and join if you can. If you are a member, or can become one, the platform provides many services and opportunities:

   - Purchasing discounts for classroom supplies, uniforms, paper products, business supplies, and more

   - Medical benefits, such as dental and vision insurance and doctors by phone

   - Teacher discounts, rebates, and other savings programs

   - A family child care toolkit, which offers resources, templates, policies, and materials specifically for family child care providers

2. Review the business pages in the "Successful Program Management" section on the ECE Shared Resources platform (typically available only to members). This category can be found on every platform and offers a vast library of materials to support the business management part of your program, such as templates for budgets, income and expense statements, business plans, and many other financial documents. You can also find links to webinars and training resources.

3. If you are a center-based provider, search for training opportunities through your state training sites, or look through the other training opportunities listed and offered on the site. If your state has a custom site, these trainings may be linked and updated from the ECE platform. Our site in New Jersey links to virtual and in-person trainings that the state offers as well as those offered by other organizations.

4. If you are a family child care provider, review your state's offerings and visit Tom Copeland's blog, *Taking Care of Business* (www.tomcopelandblog.com), for resources and webinars that are specifically designed for family child care providers.

5. Look for and join early childhood organizations to continue your professional learning, build your network, engage in professional development, and advocate for the field.

Early Childhood Organizations

Are you a member of your state AEYC or other membership organizations that offer training, resources, advocacy, and networking opportunities? If not, research which organizations will be useful to you and join them. Many organizations have several membership options and offer savings for services such as insurance, further schooling, professional development, and so on. These membership organizations also share opportunities for local engagement and advocacy, which is a crucial part of our overall work in the field and in the shared services space. Additionally, some state AEYCs manage knowledge hubs and provide access to them as a member benefit. Other types of organizations include administrator groups, infant-toddler specialty groups, literacy groups, and more. You can search online for professional organizations near you or seek opportunities through social media or other networking circles.

6. Familiarize yourself with your CCR&R and the services and resources it offers. You can find your local CCR&R at www.childcareaware.org/resources/ccrr-search. CCR&Rs have a large set of resources to support you as well as families and children. Mine offers training and programs to child care professionals; engages, registers, and supports family child care homes; oversees and manages subsidy and tuition assistance for families; serves in the role of sponsorship for the Child and Adult Care Food Program (CACFP); runs a diaper bank; and hosts many other community resources. It is also the entry point for our state's QRIS and has relationships with the centers, families, and professionals in its network. If you have an established relationship with your CCR&R, you will likely be informed when opportunities in the field arise.

7. Reach out to other alliances, early childhood stakeholders, and professionals to have conversations about opportunities that exist, and discuss possible collaborations.

8. If you are not using an automation tool for data management, tuition collection, and business tracking, this is the time to take the plunge, whether by purchasing the tools yourself or by joining a shared services alliance that will help you. Automating your business is the single biggest way for you to save money and time.

9. Seek free or low-cost training through your state licensing agencies and other state departments overseeing the early childhood education field. As well as checking for training locally, search for virtual training opportunities outside your immediate area.

10. Take advantage of the CACFP, which partially reimburses programs for meals served to children in care. There is a training and application process, as well as guidelines for qualifying and rules you must follow once enrolled. You can learn more about the CACFP through your local CCR&R, your state website, or the US Department of Agriculture (USDA) website at www.fns.usda.gov/cacfp.

11. Seek grants and other funding opportunities. Many local stores and organizations offer small grants. Your local AEYC may offer mini-grants for the Week of the Young Child or other important events. Libraries, the United Way, and other nonprofits also often support local early childhood programs.

12. Consider participating in your state subsidy program if you do not already. Each state manages its subsidy program differently. Participating in this program can help meet the needs of families in your program by making care affordable and accessible. Additionally, in some states, certain grants and other programs are open only to those programs who accept the state subsidy.

13. If it is voluntary and you are not already participating, consider joining your state's QRIS to access opportunities for your program and staff. In New Jersey, programs that participate in the Grow NJ Kids system are eligible for training and scholarships for staff and other incentives and opportunities. Additionally, some grants and opportunities are intended only for programs that participate in QRISs.

14. Seek opportunities to improve connections between elementary schools and early childhood programs. Building these relationships allows us to educate others on the importance of developmentally appropriate and play-based early education and how it positively impacts the lives of young children. These relationships may also open doors for programs to collaborate with the local school district if and when the time arises.

Mixed-Delivery Preschools

Mixed-delivery preschools have been on the rise in recent years to address the idea that one type of preschool program does not meet the needs of all children and families (Danley 2021). Mixed delivery allows school districts to operate early childhood programs without opening new classrooms in their schools. Instead, districts partner with already existing early childhood programs in the community that have established themselves as high-quality and experienced programs, providing funding and resources to existing programs and choice and quality to parents looking for care.

15. Regularly take time to research new funding and other opportunities in your state.

Taking Action

After you consider the list of opportunities above, it is time to take action. Pursuing these avenues will help ensure that you are not missing out on any grants or other resources you might qualify for. I encourage you to print the list and then do the following:

1. Make notes, do some research, and gather information from your program related to each question.

2. Identify steps you will take to realize savings wherever possible. Establish a relationship with your CCR&R, research and engage in the CACFP, and begin to work on the other items on the list to ensure that you are taking advantage of every opportunity. Even small changes add up in our industry, where we are working with such small profit margins.

The Must-Dos of Child Care Business Practices

Not all programs have the opportunity to engage in shared services in a formal way at this time, but all programs can engage in these principles to help their businesses be successful and sustainable, increase quality, and better meet the needs of the children and families in their care.

All child care businesses should do the following:

1. Analyze the program:

- What is working?

- What is not working?

- What are your goals and the desired outcomes for your program?

- Are you utilizing all available resources?

- Are you using an automation system?

2. Look for opportunities to collaborate with others regarding the following:

- Business and management services

- Resource and development sharing

- Professional development

- Advocacy

3. Look to form relationships with other colleagues and build a team that you can count on for collaboration and support.

4. Look to save time and money and to reinvest the savings into areas that help you to build a sustainable and successful business.

5. Continue to reflect and reevaluate.

6. Continue to read and learn about shared services:

- Locate your state's web platform if it exists.

- Visit the Opportunities Exchange website to learn more about shared services. It has a wealth of information, including start-up guides for networks that serve centers, multi-site centers, and family child care providers. You can benefit from the site no matter which phase of shared services implementation you are in. From finding information on how to bring shared services to your state to getting in touch with an alliance that exists and learning more about opportunities for professional development and learning, the Opportunities Exchange website is a good place to start.

If you are working as part of a shared services alliance or group, you can draw on the support and experience of others who already use some of these programs and opportunities when researching options to meet your needs individually and as a group. For example, in my current work, we have one alliance with eleven members—one child care center and ten family child care providers. Only two of the family child care providers participated in the CACFP previously. Together we evaluated the benefits of the program for the other providers, addressed whatever questions providers had and any confusion they felt surrounding the program, and supported them in deciding whether to engage in the program. They didn't have to navigate the process alone. We also identified bulk purchasing options the providers could leverage regardless of their final decision about the CACFP. This is a great example of how a shared services alliance can help programs better engage in existing opportunities that they weren't using yet and create other opportunities along the way.

Shared services is not about pointing out flaws or mistakes. It is about working collaboratively, with your team or with alliance members, to help you and your program grow and succeed. Finding your starting point gives you a direction in which to move. Remember that as early childhood leaders we are often strong pedagogical leaders, but sometimes we are missing the business leadership piece. You are not alone if you have room for improvement in one or more of the areas mentioned here. You aren't a bad leader. You are modeling for your staff and the others involved in your work how taking chances and embracing change makes us stronger.

Reinvesting in Your Child Care Business

While engaging in shared services allows you to save time and money in your program, the more important reason to participate in shared services is that it allows you to reinvest those resources in areas that are important to you and your vision. Shared services gives you the opportunity to do things that may have been on your to-do list but you've never had the chance to complete, such as the following:

Pursuing Quality Improvement

Shared services can introduce you to opportunities for improving the quality of your program, such as through a national accreditation system, your state QRIS, or through another identified resource; it can also help you reorganize so that you have enough time to pursue these opportunities.

Reinvesting in the Workforce

The workforce of child care and early childhood education has long faced a grim outlook. Since the onset of the COVID-19 pandemic, there has been increased focus on the low wages and inadequate support our staff receive. Although early educators are often highly educated, they are often paid minimum wage and not viewed as essential to children's development. Early childhood education is losing workers to other industries that offer better pay and benefits and have a less stressful work environment. Reinvesting in our programs allows us to pay our staff a higher wage. By saving money and time in identified areas, we can reinvest some of these dollars into our staff. Increasing wages and benefits are crucial steps to securing our educators' commitment and the future of the field.

Building Bridges and Advocating for Change on a Larger Stage

Engaging in shared services helps providers build relationships with peers and outside organizations, opening a path to advocacy work. We can call attention to the many benefits of early childhood education, the importance of the jobs early educators do, the dedication and worth of these educators, and the importance of providing them a respectful wage and other benefits on par with educators of older children. Together we can do the following:

- Create opportunities that otherwise might not exist

- Offer benefits and other resources that otherwise wouldn't be possible

- Spotlight the work and qualifications of our workforce

- Advocate for change

We are stronger together. We can bring change and sustainable outcomes to the workforce and our programs, and this in turn benefits the children and families in our care.

CHAPTER 8
THE BIG PICTURE

I spent the first chapters of this book talking about the history of child care and the issues that have faced our field for many years. I think it is important, therefore, to end this book with a look back at these topics. The issues are large but not insurmountable:

- There is a substantial need for access to quality and affordable child care.

- We have a crisis surrounding recruiting and retaining a workforce in a society where the profession is inadequately respected and compensated.

- Many people fail to view the time of early development and the work of early childhood programs as meaningful in children's lives.

- Many people do not understand the importance of providing developmentally appropriate and high-quality early education opportunities to all children in a format that meets their individual needs.

- Overall, the profession is foundational to society yet is not viewed as such.

One way we make progress is by rebuilding our child care programs with strong business practices so we have a sustainable model for our future chapters. We can do this by using the tool of shared services. By utilizing this opportunity, individual providers can build strong business and pedagogical practices and better meet the needs of their program, their staff, and the children and families they serve. Shared services affords us the opportunity to learn from our past and build a sustainable future for all.

To see the whole picture, we must first rebuild the foundation.

I spend a portion of my work each week doing repairs on this foundation, repeating to the providers on our team that they are not babysitters but small-business owners, reminding them that they should carry this title proudly. Whether they own and operate a multisite program or a family child care program, they are business leaders. These businesses are often women- and minority-owned or operated. Some owners are single parents themselves, living on an ALICE budget, and they mirror the low-income or ALICE families they regularly serve. They face disrespect as small-business owners and leaders because their work has traditionally not been valued—but they should be proud. The time for change is now.

Our foundation building starts here.

Our future starts here.

We support one another. We see our worth.

We build connections. We collaborate.

We grow our knowledge base. We strengthen our business skills. We improve quality.

We reimagine our work, our programs, our systems. We reimagine ourselves.

We advocate for change.

We grow. We set goals and work together to meet them.

We build our confidence, our experiences, and our programs.

We educate others, increase the quality of the care we provide, and increase access and affordability through our efforts.

We lead.

Whether this book was your first step on the road of shared services or another stop along a road you have been traveling for a while, I challenge you to keep walking forward. Use this book as a catalyst to strengthen your steps and your resolve as we work to make shared services a part of our daily work, our program models, and our industry, in a collaborative and hands-on manner.

APPENDIX A
IRON TRIANGLE
PLANNING WORKSHEET

The Iron Triangle of Early Childhood Programs

After reading about the iron triangle in chapter 5, use the chart below to make notes about the steps you can take in each category.

Full Enrollment	Full Fee Collection	Revenue Covers Cost per Child

APPENDIX B
TIME-SAVING GOALS WORKSHEET

1. For one week, keep a daily log of your work activities. The list should be comprehensive, almost as if you were keeping a food journal or a mindfulness journal.

2. From your list, identify the activities and commitments to which you would like to dedicate more time.

3. From your list, identify things that you would like to delegate, automate, or contract out to others.

4. Begin researching automation and outside contractor options. Don't forget to check for your state's shared services offerings, including knowledge hubs and alliances, to assist in this research and to find other ideas for saving time.

5. To whom in your program could you delegate the tasks you identified above to allow you to focus on your list of priorities?

Staff Member	Tasks to Be Delegated

6. What tasks could you automate?

Task	Plan to Automate

7. What activities could you contract out if they cannot be delegated or automated?

Task	Plan to Contract This Task Out

8. Create deadlines to delegate, contract out, or automate the tasks listed above.

9. Make a plan to insert the items you wish to dedicate more time to into your daily schedule and to-do lists. Talk about this plan with your staff so that you can hold one another accountable.

APPENDIX C
MONEY-SAVING
PLANNING WORKSHEET

Identifying areas where you can save money in your program is an important step to sustainability. Answer the following questions to begin this journey.

Tuition Collection

1. Do you have a rate sheet for families that identifies tuition rates as well as extra fees that will be assessed?

2. Do you have an enrollment agreement?

3. Do you have written policies for fee collection, assessment, and collection?

4. Do you use automated tuition collection software?

5. Have you used the Iron Triangle Planning Worksheet to identify areas for improvement in your operations?

Payroll

1. Are you using a payroll-processing system?

2. Is a time card system part of your child care management service (CCMS)?

3. Do you have policies and procedures for payroll, time off, and so on?

4. Can you make a list of steps to look for savings in this area?

Marketing

1. Do you have a marketing plan?

2. Do you market in various ways over multiple mediums?

3. Do you have a system to keep track of leads?

4. Do you engage with potential clients who choose not to enroll in your program?

5. What are your marketing goals for this year?

Food Purchasing/Prep/Service

1. Have you investigated whether participating in the Child and Adult Care Food Program (CACFP) would be beneficial to your program?

2. Do you serve food in your program? Would this be a benefit to your program?

3. Would a bulk purchasing system help you to save money in this area? Would a meal prep plan help you save on the amount of time that you spend cooking and preparing meals?

4. Would it be helpful to engage in shared services in this area—for example, with a shared shopper, a food service staff person, or other ideas?

Materials and Other Purchasing Plans

1. Do you have a plan for saving money on your purchases?

2. Can you engage in a shared services arrangement with other programs to realize a discounted rate?

3. What other creative ideas can you discover to save money in purchasing? Can you engage with a shared services group to brainstorm savings ideas?

Human Resources

1. Does your payroll company provide and update a staff manual? If you do not have a staff manual with policies and procedures, creating one is a necessary step.

2. Do you use multiple methods to communicate with staff regarding policies, procedures, and expectations?

3. Do you offer benefits to your staff? If not, research creative ways to provide benefits.

4. To what extent do you create a workplace culture that conveys worth, respect, and professionalism within the program?

Business Expenses

1. Do you utilize professional services? If so, have you connected with other program leaders to search for cost savings where possible?

2. Can you bundle services in this area?

3. Can you make a list of your business expenses and brainstorm ways to save money in this area?

Use the space below to brainstorm other areas where you would like to investigate savings within your program.

Use the space below to brainstorm ideas to help you improve your procedures for staff recruitment and retention.

Use the space below to brainstorm other ideas for saving money.

APPENDIX D
OPPORTUNITIES CHECKLIST

Be sure to look for existing resources and opportunities that you are not taking advantage of yet. You can use the list below to locate and keep track of opportunities in your area.

1. Visit your local ECE Shared Resources platform. If you do not have an account, see how you can become a member and join if you can. If you are a member, or can become one, the platform provides many services and opportunities:

   - Purchasing discounts for classroom supplies, uniforms, paper products, business supplies, and more

   - Medical benefits, such as dental and vision insurance and doctors by phone

   - Teacher discounts, rebates, and other savings programs

   - A family child care toolkit, which offers resources, templates, policies, and materials specifically for family child care providers

2. Review the business pages in the "Successful Program Management" section on the ECE Shared Resources platform (typically available only to members). This category can be found on every platform and offers a vast library of materials to support the business management part of your program, such as templates for budgets, income and expense statements, business plans, and many other financial documents. You can also find links to webinars and training resources.

3. If you are a center-based provider, search for training opportunities through your state training sites or look through the other training opportunities listed and offered on the site. If your state has a custom site, these trainings may be linked and updated from the ECE platform. Our site in New Jersey links to virtual and in-person trainings that the state offers as well as those offered by other organizations.

4. If you are a family child care provider, review your state's offerings and visit Tom Copeland's blog, *Taking Care of Business* (www.tomcopelandblog.com), for resources and webinars that are specifically designed for family child care providers.

5. Look for and join early childhood organizations to continue your professional learning, build your network, engage in professional development, and advocate for the field.

Early Childhood Organizations

Are you a member of your state AEYC or other membership organizations that offer training, resources, advocacy, and networking opportunities? If not, research which organizations will be useful to you and join them. Many organizations have several membership options and offer savings for services such as insurance, further schooling, professional development, and so on. These membership organizations also share opportunities for local engagement and advocacy, which is a crucial part of our overall work in the field and in the shared services space. Additionally, some state AEYCs manage knowledge hubs and provide access to them as a member benefit. Other types of organizations include administrator groups, infant-toddler specialty groups, literacy groups, and more. You can search online for professional organizations near you or seek opportunities through social media or other networking circles.

---

6. Familiarize yourself with your CCR&R and the services and resources it offers. You can find your local CCR&R at www.childcareaware.org/resources/ccrr-search. CCR&Rs have a large set of resources to support you as well as families and children. Mine offers training and programs to child care professionals; engages, registers, and supports family child care homes; oversees and manages subsidy and tuition assistance for families; serves in the role of sponsorship for the Child and Adult Care Food Program (CACFP); runs a diaper bank; and hosts many other community resources. It is also the entry point for our state's QRIS and has relationships with the centers, families, and professionals in its network. If you have an established relationship with your CCR&R, you will likely be informed when opportunities in the field arise.

7. Reach out to other alliances, early childhood stakeholders, and professionals to have conversations about opportunities that exist, and discuss possible collaborations.

8. If you are not using an automation tool for data management, tuition collection, and business tracking, this is the time to take the plunge, whether by purchasing the tools yourself or by joining a shared services alliance that will help you. Automating your business is the single biggest way for you to save money and time.

9. Seek free or low-cost training through your state licensing agencies and other state departments overseeing the early childhood education field. As well as checking for training locally, search for virtual training opportunities outside your immediate area.

10. Take advantage of the CACFP, which partially reimburses programs for meals served to children in care. There is a training and application process, as well as guidelines for qualifying and rules you must follow once enrolled. You can learn more about the CACFP through your local CCR&R, your state website, or the US Department of Agriculture (USDA) website at www.fns.usda.gov/cacfp.

11. Seek grants and other funding opportunities. Many local stores and organizations offer small grants. Your local AEYC may offer mini-grants for the Week of the Young Child or other important events. Libraries, the United Way, and other nonprofits also often support local early childhood programs.

12. Consider participating in your state subsidy program if you do not already. Each state manages its subsidy program differently. Participating in this program can help meet the needs of families in your program by making care affordable and accessible. Additionally, in some states, certain grants and other programs are open only to those programs who accept the state subsidy.

13. If it is voluntary and you are not already participating, consider joining your state's QRIS to access opportunities for your program and staff. In New Jersey, programs that participate in the Grow NJ Kids system are eligible for training and scholarships for staff and other incentives and opportunities. Additionally, some grants and opportunities are intended only for programs that participate in QRISs.

14. Seek opportunities to improve connections between elementary schools and early childhood programs. Building these relationships allows us to educate others on the importance of developmentally appropriate and play-based early education and how it positively impacts the lives of young children. These relationships may also open doors for programs to collaborate with the local school district if and when the time arises.

Mixed-Delivery Preschools

Mixed-delivery preschools have been on the rise in recent years to address the idea that one type of preschool program does not meet the needs of all children and families (Danley 2021). Mixed delivery allows school districts to operate early childhood programs without opening new classrooms in their schools. Instead, districts partner with already existing early childhood programs in the community that have established themselves as high-quality and experienced programs, providing funding and resources to existing programs and choice and quality to parents looking for care.

---

15. Regularly take time to research new funding and other opportunities in your state.

RESOURCES

Useful Links to Learn More About or Engage in Shared Services

Build Initiative—https://buildinitiative.org/work/quality-improvement

Child Care Aware of America—www.childcareaware.org

Child Care Technical Assistance Network—https://childcareta.acf.hhs.gov

ECE Shared Resources—www.ecesharedresources.com

Opportunities Exchange—www.oppex.org

Taking Care of Business—http://tomcopelandblog.com

CCA for Social Good—www.ccaglobalpartners.com/divisions/cca-for-social-good

Useful Websites on Related Topics

Child and Adult Care Food Program (CACFP)—www.fns.usda.gov/cacfp

First Five Years Fund—www.ffyf.org

National Association for the Education of Young Children (NAEYC)—www.naeyc.org

Zero to Three—www.zerotothree.org

REFERENCES

Bleiweis, Robin, Jocelyn Frye, and Rose Khattar. 2021. "Women of Color and the Wage Gap." Center for American Progress. Last modified November 17, 2021. www.americanprogress .org/article/women-of-color-and-the-wage-gap.

Center on the Developing Child at Harvard University. n.d. "Brain Architecture." Accessed September 9, 2022. https://developingchild.harvard.edu/science/key-concepts /brain-architecture.

Danley, Lucy. 2021. "Mixed Delivery Systems Encourage Parent Choice and Strengthen Child Care Programs." Published June 24, 2021. First Five Years Fund. www.ffyf.org /mixed-delivery-systems-encourage-parent-choice-and-strengthen-child-care-programs.

ECE Shared Resources. n.d. "Partners & Impact." Accessed November 27, 2021. www.ecesharedresources.com/working-with-us/partners-impact.

HHS (US Department of Health and Human Services). 2022. "Annual Update of the HHS Poverty Guidelines." *Federal Register* 87 (14): 3315–16. https://aspe.hhs.gov/topics /poverty-economic-mobility/poverty-guidelines.

McLean, Caitlin, Lea J. E. Austin, Marcy Whitebook, and Krista L. Olson. 2020. *Early Childhood Workforce Index 2020*. Center for the Study of Child Care Employment. https://cscce .berkeley.edu/workforce-index-2020.

Opportunities Exchange. n.d. "Local and State Alliances." Accessed September 7, 2022. www .oppex.org/local-state-alliances.

Stoney, Louise. 2010. *The Iron Triangle: A Simple Formula for Financial Policy in ECE Programs*. Opportunities Exchange. www.oppex.org/s/OppEx_2021_IronTriangle.pdf.

Talan, Teri, and Marina Magid. 2021. *Closing the Leadership Gap: 2021 Status Update on Early Childhood Program Leadership in the United States*. Wheeling, IL: McCormick Center for Early Childhood Leadership. https://mccormickcenter.nl.edu/library/closing-the -leadership-gap-113021.

United for ALICE. 2018. "United for ALICE Wage Tool." Last modified 2018. www.unitedforalice .org/wage-tool.

CPSIA information can be obtained
at www.ICGtesting.com
Printed in the USA
JSHW061214180123
36272JS00004B/6

9 781605 547879